C000258932

the little book of
BAD HAIR DAYS

the little book of BAD HAIR DAYS

Raymond Glynne

ARCTURUS

ARCTURUS

This edition published in 2012 by Arcturus Publishing Limited
26/27 Bickels Yard, 151–153 Bermondsey Street,
London SE1 3HA

ISBN: 978-1-84858-372-6
AD002101EN

Printed in China

'**D**'ya ever get one of them days?' asked Elvis Presley. 'When nothing goes right from morning till night, d'ya ever get one of them days?' It seems that even the King was prone to the occasional **Bad Hair Day**.

Call it bio-rhythms, call it the stars, call it getting out of bed on the wrong side; whatever the reason, we all have days when things just refuse to fall into place.

And there's only one cure for a **Bad Hair Day**: give up and go back to bed!

We can't always expect to be on top form.

There are days when everything looks bleak.

Nothing you do seems to work.

And people seem to want to make your life hell.

That's what you call a Bad Hair Day!

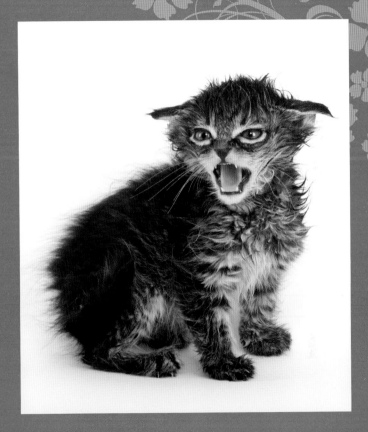

**You know it's a Bad Hair Day when the sight
of your own face scares you.**

You know those days when things don't quite fall into place?

**When even putting on your best outfit fails
to lift the spirits.**

As the eyes focus, the mouth breaks into a wail.

And as realization dawns, despair sets in.

I CAN'T GO OUT THERE!

On Bad Hair Days we try to hide ourselves away.

I'm going to stay in and ride this one out.

We choose to drift alone through the darkening void.

The world seems a terrifying place.

No! Don't make me go out there!

You can often tell when someone's having a **Bad Hair Day.**

Oops! This one's looking for trouble.

I said NO MORE PICTURES!

Try me. Just try me.

Back off, everybody. I think she's going to blow!

Not happy.

Not happy at all.

In fact, I'm really rather cross.

You think I'm going to forget this in a hurry.

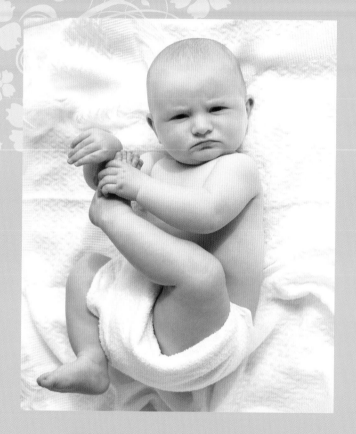

I'll be having words with you later.

I don't think it's nice, you laughing.

You can run, but you can't hide.

Do you feel lucky? Well? Do ya… punk?

Are you looking at me? Are YOU looking at ME?

Do you want a piece of me?

Everybody fears that look of self-righteous outrage.

I'm not sulking – you are!

Is that steam coming out of your ears?

That indignant stare can burn right through you.

And what's worse, it seems to be catching.

Why does everyone and everything have to
try your patience so much?

Please make it go away.

Aaaaaaaaagh!

I sometimes wonder if I'm the only intelligent creature
on the planet.

Typical!

I CAN'T TAKE ANY MORE!

We all have our breaking point.

Complete physical and mental exhaustion.

Sometimes it makes us scream.

Other times we just bury our head in our hands.

Mr Bear has left the building.

This camel's got the hump.

We've all seen it: the grumpy refusal to budge.

It's the ultimate protest when all argument fails.

We can see you're going to take some shifting.

It's a sit-down protest, is it?

I suppose you think that's funny.

I'm definitely going back to bed.

Hmm? What's eating Arthur?

That's right. Everybody have a good laugh.

Oh, hilarious!

Sometimes you couldn't care less what people say.

Does this face look bothered?

Frankly, my dear, I don't give a damn!

Ya boo sucks!

La la la la la la la la.

Sometimes we just have to get away.

Slip quietly into the background and mope.

Take time alone to contemplate the injustice of life.

Wonder why nobody understands.

And torture ourselves with our own cold thoughts.

Beware the temptation to drown your sorrows.

I need a drink.

I know I shouldn't, but I find it helps.

Resist. Resist. Re… Give in.

You could end up worse than when you started.

Coo, there's just no pleasing some people.

I really can't see what more I could do for them.

Maybe if I pretend to be dead they'll leave me alone.

I'm spent.

Count me out, I'm finished!

Of course, the number one cause of **Bad Hair Days** is... bad hair.

THAT'S THE LAST TIME I GO TO THAT SALON!

So that's a blow dry?

I'm not even going to show you what they did to me...

Do you think it was their idea of a joke?

Well, I don't think it's 'cute'.

A change of style isn't always a good idea.

The wrong look can knock us off our perch.

Yes? No? Back to the drawing board.

I dunno, it feels kinda impractical.

I think I need to shave it all off and start again.

But don't let a Bad Hair Day hold you back.

**What might look like a disaster to others
could actually take your fancy.**

Yeah! I like this look.

**Makes me look kinda mean,
doncha think?**

Chin up, son. They're only jealous.